Julie

JUST FOR
FUN

The make-it, play-it, solve-it book of fun!

★ American Girl®

Published by American Girl Publishing, Inc.
Copyright © 2009 by American Girl, LLC

Questions or comments? Call 1-800-845-0005,
visit our Web site at americangirl.com, or write to Customer Service,
American Girl, 8400 Fairway Place, Middleton, WI 53562-0497.

Printed in China
10 11 12 13 14 15 16 LEO 10 9 8 7 6 5 4 3 2

Written by Jodi Goldberg
Designed by Susan Walsh
Produced by Jeannette Bailey, Julie Kimmell, Judith Lary,
Gail Longworth, Kendra Schluter, and Mark Speltz
Cover Illustration by Robert Hunt
Interior Illustrations by Robert Hunt, Nika Korniyenko, and Susan McAliley

Table of Contents

Sticker Sudoku

Solve the Sudoku puzzle by using the picture stickers of Julie's family and friends. Fill in the boxes so that every row, every column, and every 2-by-3 rectangle has one of each of the six characters.

These stickers are reusable, so you can move them around as you work the puzzle. When you've solved the Sudoku, remove the stickers and pass on the puzzle to a friend.

San Francisco Scramble

How many different words can you make from the letters that spell Julie's hometown of "San Francisco"? Check the answer section to see how many we came up with.

SAN FRANCISCO

Shopping Switch-Up

Julie and her best friend, Ivy, had a blast shopping in San Francisco's Chinatown. The stores were crammed from top to bottom with all sorts of exotic treasures. Can you find ten details in the picture on the right that are different from those in the picture on the left?

Make a Cootie Catcher

Julie and her friend Ivy made cootie catchers to tell their fortunes. Punch out the cootie catcher on page 11 and follow the directions to make your own.

  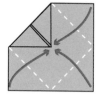

1 Fold each corner point into the center.

2 Flip so that the flaps are face-down. Fold each corner into the center.

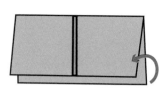

3 Fold in half to crease.

4 Unfold, and fold in half the other way.

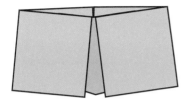

5 Stick your thumbs and first two fingers into the four pockets. Push all the pockets to the center to begin playing.

TO USE:

1. Pick a word on top of the cootie catcher.

2. Open and close the center points the same number of times as the letters in the word, alternating sides.

3. Pick a number. Open and close the center points as many times as the number.

4. Pick another number. Open the flap and read your fortune.

Groovy

1 You will be the voice of an animated character on TV.

2 You'll live in a city on the top floor of a high-rise building.

3 You will choreograph a new Broadway show.

4 You'll write a best-selling novel for girls.

5 You will win a karaoke contest at a friend's party.

6 You will always know the perfect gifts for your friends.

7 You'll make the biggest splash at a pool party.

8 You will eat too many cupcakes on your next birthday.

Far Out!

Bake Zucchini Bread

When Julie and her family moved into their new apartment,
a friendly neighbor welcomed them with homemade zucchini bread.
The bread was so moist and sweet that Julie barely noticed
she was eating vegetables!

Zucchini Bread

Ingredients

- Butter, shortening, or cooking spray
- 3 eggs
- 2 cups firmly packed light brown sugar
- 1 cup vegetable oil
- 2 teaspoons vanilla
- 2 cups flour
- 1 teaspoon salt
- 1 teaspoon baking powder
- 1 teaspoon baking soda
- 2 teaspoons cinnamon
- 2 cups grated zucchini (2–3 medium zucchini)
- 1 cup chopped walnuts (optional)

Equipment

- Paper towels
- Two 9-by-5-inch loaf pans
- Large mixing bowl
- Measuring cups and spoons
- Electric mixer
- Sifter
- Medium mixing bowl
- Rubber spatula
- Vegetable peeler
- Grater
- Wooden spoon
- Toothpick
- Pot holders
- Table knife
- Wire cooling racks

✋⭐ Have an adult help you with all the steps in this recipe.

1. Preheat the oven to 325°. Use the paper towels to grease the loaf pans with butter or shortening, or coat the pans with cooking spray.

2. Crack the eggs into the large mixing bowl. Add the brown sugar, oil, and vanilla. Use the electric mixer on medium speed to beat the ingredients until combined.

3. Put the sifter into the medium mixing bowl. Measure the flour, salt, baking powder, baking soda, and cinnamon into the sifter, and sift them into the bowl.

4. Add half of the flour mixture to the egg mixture. Use the mixer on medium speed to combine the ingredients. Turn off the mixer and scrape the sides of the bowl with the rubber spatula. Add the rest of the flour mixture and beat just until combined.

5. Peel* and grate the zucchini. Measure 2 cups and add it to the batter. Add the nuts and stir gently with the wooden spoon.

6. Pour the batter into the loaf pans, dividing it evenly between the two pans. Put the pans into the oven.

7. Bake the loaves for 1 hour. Poke a toothpick into the center of one of the loaves. If the toothpick comes out clean, the bread is done. If not, bake 5 more minutes and test again. When the bread is

done, remove it from the oven.

8. Let the loaves cool in the pans for 10 minutes. Run a knife along the sides of the pans to loosen the bread. Remove the bread from the pans and cool completely on wire racks.

*You can leave the peel on the zucchini if you like. If you do, the bread will be green.

Zucchini bread freezes well. After the loaf has cooled completely, wrap it in a layer of plastic wrap and then a layer of aluminum foil. Freeze it for up to 3 months. To thaw the bread, place the wrapped loaf in the refrigerator for a day. Unwrap it, slice it, and enjoy.

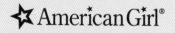

Draw Nutmeg

Julie's pet rabbit, Nutmeg, likes to eat apple peels and snuggle in bed with Julie. Follow these step-by-step instructions to learn how to draw Nutmeg.

Use a pencil for steps 1 through 5. For step 6, use markers, crayons, or colored pencils. Use a fine-tip black marker to outline the drawing when you're finished.

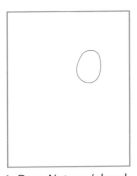

1. Draw Nutmeg's head.

2. Now add droopy ears.

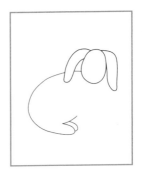

3. Draw her back, belly, and hind legs.

4. Next come her front legs.

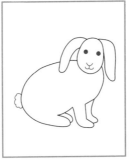

5. A nose, two eyes, a mouth, and a tail give her personality.

6. Complete the picture of Nutmeg by making her a soft brown color.

Picture Yourself in a Catalogue

How would you look wearing fashionable outfits and hairstyles from the 1970s? Find out! Tear out the facing page and remove the blank faces from each illustration. Slip your photo behind the illustration and tape the photo in place. Try pictures of your friends and relatives, too.

Bookmarks

Bookmarks to tear and share

★ American Girl®

★ American Girl®

★ American Girl®

★ American Girl®

Shopping at Gladrags

Julie's mom opened a shop called Gladrags that sold trendy clothes, jewelry, toys, and accessories. Can you find the names of the groovy things Mom sold? The words are hidden backward, forward, diagonally, and up and down. Some letters will be used for more than one word.

```
C T B N J U P F Q R H B O P E
M E Y D Y A C T K I E E B E V
T R B J H J I C R A B G I A X
X R G A T Q O F D H G P Y S S
N A O K N R V C P C O J U A J
Q R I L T D U T G G V N G N P
U I I E L R A X T A R Y O T M
H U P S T D Y N K B L I Y B A
D M L A B E O M N N K H D L L
P G I O H T J L Q A Y J X O A
G N I R D O O M L E S G U U V
S D A W E N R V Y B L K I S A
G U R T O O F Y Z Z U F I E L
B L U E J E A N P U R S E R P
N T I E D Y E D T S H I R T T
```

BANDANNA SKIRT

BEAD CURTAINS

BEANBAG CHAIR

BLUE-JEAN PURSE

FUZZY FOOT RUG

LAVA LAMP

MOOD RING

PEASANT BLOUSE

PET ROCK

TERRARIUM

TIE-DYED T-SHIRT

TROLL DOLL

Eagle Rescue

When Julie learned that bald eagles were losing their homes and their lives all across California, what did she decide to do about it?

To solve the puzzle, place the letters above the purple line in the boxes below the purple line to form words. The letters in each column can be used only in that column. An orange square indicates the end of a word.

C	T	H	L	D	E	S	O	I	H	E	L	R
M	O	U	E	Y	T	T	A	D	S	S	E	P
C	L	H	E	S		O	O	L	T	H	E	
	O	A	E			A			E	H		

	S					L					
			S									Y
				R								
		N								E		
					G						

Two Different Dinners

Julie, Tracy, and Mom got Chinese takeout their first night in their new apartment. These two pictures are almost the same. Find ten things in the bottom picture that are different from those in the top picture.

Julie's Bedroom

Decorate Julie's room with these removable, reusable stickers.

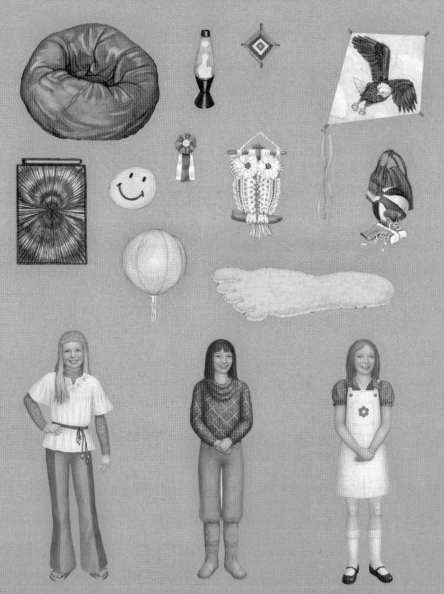

Twists and Turns

For Julie's best friend, Ivy, the best part of the day was her afternoon spent practicing gymnastics at the YWCA. Fit the gymnastics moves and equipment in the cross grid according to word length.

Start by filling in the 3- and 13-letter words. There's only one place each of those words will fit. Then fill in the rest of the puzzle.

3 letters
MAT

4 letters
BEAM
PLIÉ

5 letters
MOUNT
PIVOT
VAULT

8 letters
BACKFLIP
DISMOUNT
ROUND OFF
TUCK JUMP

9 letters
CARTWHEEL
SPLIT JUMP
STRETCHES

10 letters
PIROUETTES
SOMERSAULT
UNEVEN BARS

13 letters
FLOOR EXERCISE

Chinese New Year Feast

Ivy invited Julie's whole family to celebrate Chinese New Year at her grandparents' restaurant, The Happy Panda. Julie worried that her sister, Tracy, wouldn't like all the new and different foods.

Unscramble the words to find out what was on the menu for the Chinese New Year feast. Then find the foods in the puzzle on the right.

bird's nest puos   ____ ____ ____ ____

cire   ____ ____ ____ ____

long life oondsle   ____ ____ ____ ____ ____ ____ ____

umdpligns   ____ ____ ____ ____ ____ ____ ____ ____ __

ate   ____ ____ ____

lmadon cookies   ____ ____ ____ ____ ____ ____

fortune osokcie   ____ ____ ____ ____ ____ ____ ____

chinese bagbace   ____ ____ ____ ____ ____ ____ ____

bitter enlom   ____ ____ ____ ____ ____

wood ear usomhrom   ____ ____ ____ ____ ____ ____ ____ ____

anngterie   ____ ____ ____ ____ ____ ____ ____ ____ ____

red melon sesde   ____ ____ ____ ____ ____

iadncde fruit   ____ ____ ____ ____ ____ ____ ____

egg llors   ____ ____ ____ ____ ____

ufot   ____ ____ ____ ____

```
Q  V  E  A  T  C  M  D  Q  S  T  Y  P  X  A  M  X  V
O  D  U  P  K  P  A  O  V  I  G  N  U  T  O  F  U  Z
P  K  R  N  Y  Y  M  N  O  N  W  N  O  M  I  J  N  N
S  D  E  E  S  E  N  L  D  R  N  G  S  A  V  C  G  S
S  G  N  I  L  P  M  U  D  I  H  G  T  X  H  E  S  A
D  N  W  O  T  Z  S  L  U  Y  E  S  R  V  R  P  E  L
L  Z  N  Q  L  E  N  F  T  W  K  D  U  I  J  A  L  M
M  E  I  C  I  F  Z  D  K  R  Y  S  N  M  J  K  D  O
U  K  D  K  R  R  T  L  T  Z  D  E  L  K  P  J  O  N
B  G  O  C  A  B  B  A  G  E  T  G  O  L  Z  C  O  D
R  O  P  Q  Z  O  H  P  C  D  A  G  H  Q  O  B  N  R
C  T  D  Z  A  X  J  I  E  A  Q  J  Y  M  D  R  J  O
J  Q  A  D  D  T  R  O  W  E  N  I  R  E  G  N  A  T
```

No Way!

Smiley faces were a sunny symbol of the 1970s. Punch out these cute cards, and then play "No Way!" with 3 to 6 friends.

Goal: Be the first to bluff all your cards away.

Setup: The dealer shuffles the deck and deals all the cards. Players sort their cards by rank, creating a pile with the lowest on top. Hold your cards.

How to Play:

1. The player to the dealer's left goes first. She has to start with 2s. She can choose whether or not to *bluff*, or try to fool the other players. As she lays down her 2s in a neat stack, facedown, she calls out what she's playing. For example, she says, "Three 2s."

2. Now the other players must decide whether or not they think she's bluffing. Hint: Look at your cards. If you already have two 2s in your hand, it's impossible for her to have three 2s.

3. If a girl thinks the first player is bluffing, she challenges her by yelling "No way!" Then the first player has to turn her cards faceup. (If two girls yell "No way!" at the same time, the girl closest to the player's left is the challenger.)

4. If the player was telling the truth, the challenger has to take the cards. If she was bluffing, she has to take her cards back. Her turn is over.

5. If no one challenges the first player, the cards stay facedown on the table. The next player who loses a challenge has to take all the cards on the table.

6. The game continues in the same way. The next player lays down 3s, the player after her lays down 4s, and so on. After the aces, start with 2s again.

7. The first player to get rid of all her cards wins!

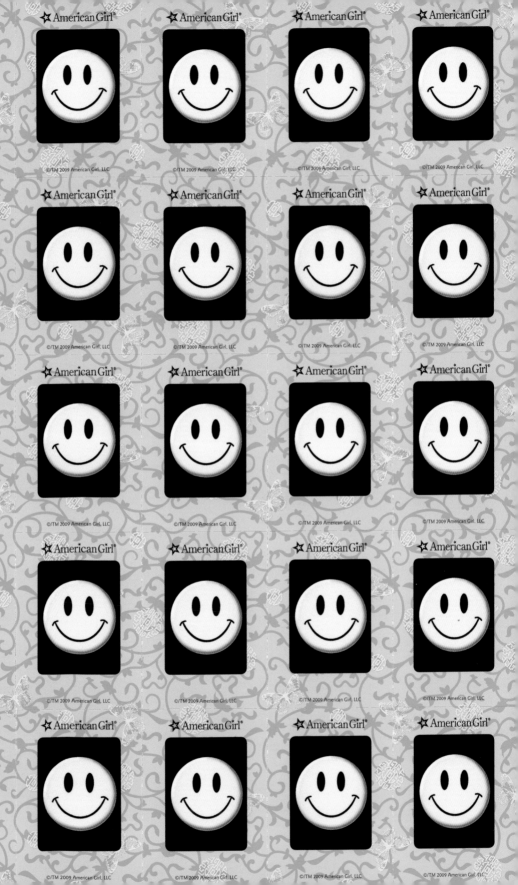

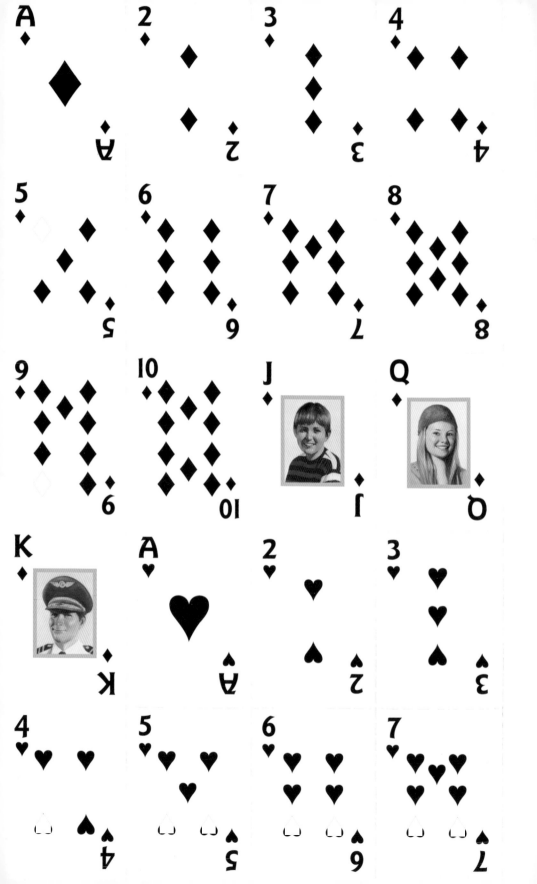

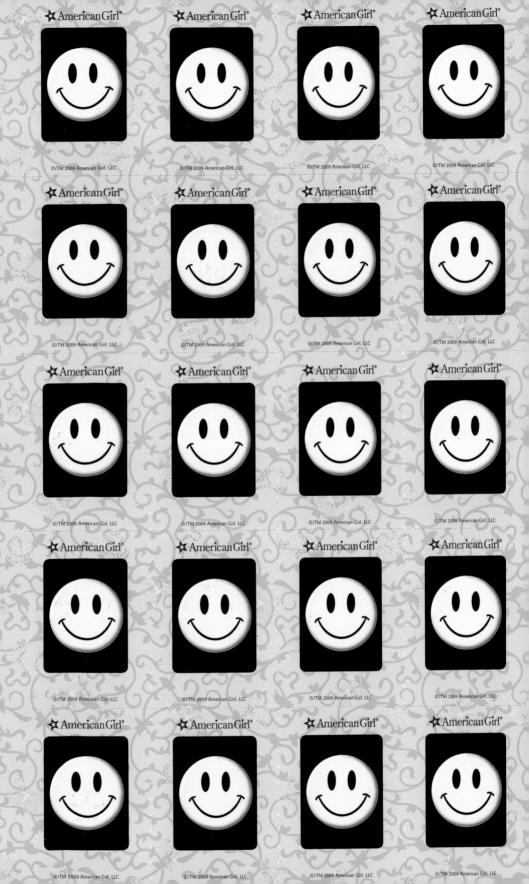

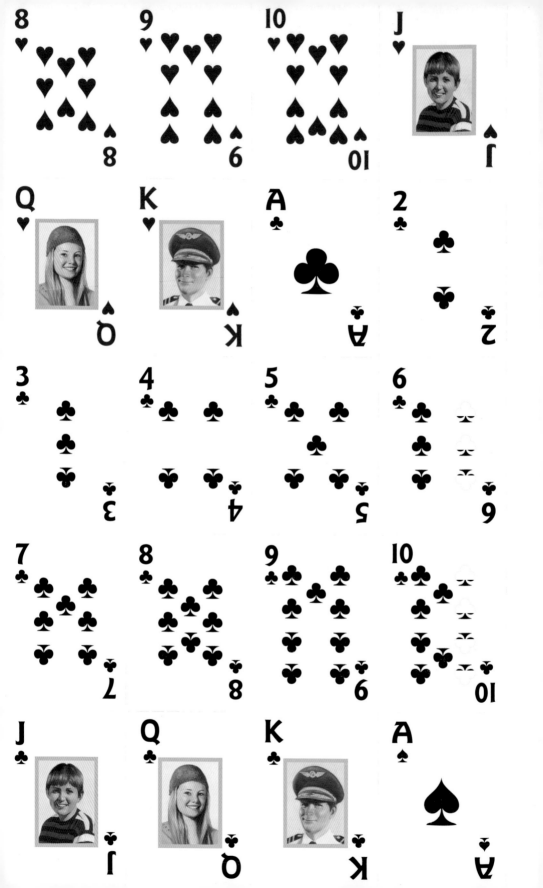

©/TM 2009 American Girl, LLC
©/TM 2009 American Girl, LLC
©/TM 2009 American Girl, LLC
©/TM 2009 American Girl, LLC

©/TM 2009 American Girl, LLC
©/TM 2009 American Girl, LLC
©/TM 2009 American Girl, LLC
©/TM 2009 American Girl, LLC

©/TM 2009 American Girl, LLC
©/TM 2009 American Girl, LLC
©/TM 2009 American Girl, LLC
©/TM 2009 American Girl, LLC

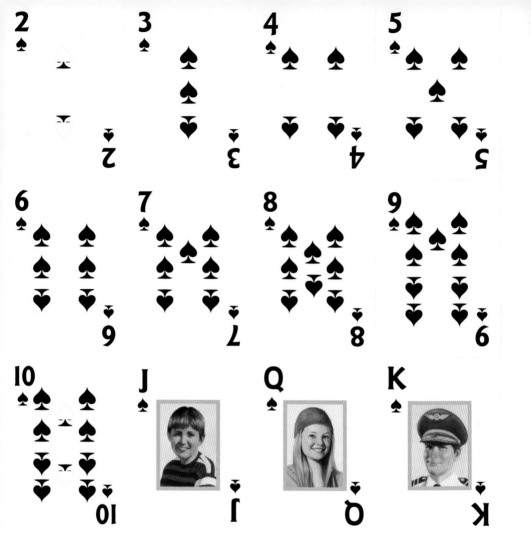

Draw a Bald Eagle

Julie leads the charge in raising money to release two bald eagles and their chick safely into the wild. Follow these step-by-step directions to draw your own eagle.

Use a pencil for steps 1 through 5. For step 6, use markers, crayons, or colored pencils. Use a fine-tip black marker to outline the drawing when you're finished.

1. Draw the eagle wing and upper body.

2. Now add a head, neck, and tail feathers.

3. Draw her eyes, beak, and legs.

4. Next come her feet, feathers, and wing line.

5. Tail feathers, talons, and an eye pupil give her personality.

6. Finally, complete the picture of the eagle by coloring her.

Word Race

Here's a puzzle to play with a friend. Punch out the two game cards. Set a timer for 2 to 5 minutes. See how many different words each of you can make from the letters in the word "Bicentennial." When time is up, compare your lists. Cross out any words that are on both lists, and then score the remaining words by giving the following points:

2 letters = 1 point

3 letters = 2 points

4 letters = 3 points

5 or more letters = 4 points

Check the answer section to see which words we came up with.

BICENTENNIAL

_____   _____

_____   _____

_____   _____

_____   _____

_____   _____

_____   _____

_____   _____

_____   _____

BICENTENNIAL

_____   _____

_____   _____

_____   _____

_____   _____

_____   _____

_____   _____

_____   _____

BICENTENNIAL

_____   _____

_____   _____

_____   _____

_____   _____

_____   _____

_____   _____

_____   _____

_____   _____

BICENTENNIAL

_____   _____

_____   _____

_____   _____

_____   _____

_____   _____

_____   _____

_____   _____

Lost in Chinatown!

Julie and Ivy got separated from Ivy's mother in Chinatown and now they're lost! Help them find Ivy's mother at the fortune cookie factory.

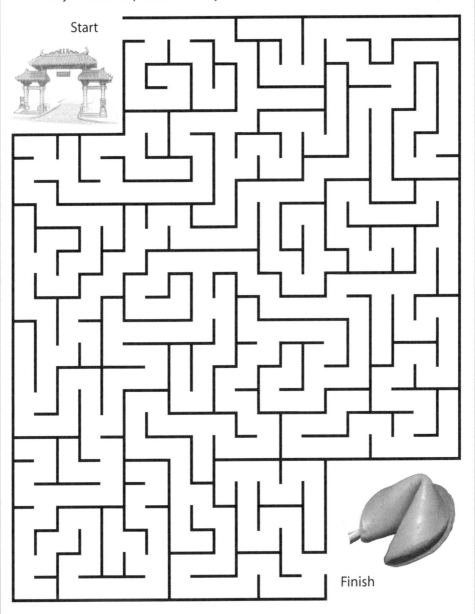

Start

Finish

Make a Paper Butterfly

In the 1970s, girls did origami and other paper crafts. Julie loved animals and anything to do with nature, so she might have enjoyed decorating her room with these paper butterflies. Here's how to make your own:

Materials

Origami paper (see next page)

Colored masking tape, ¼" to ⅜" wide

Glue Dots or glue stick

Embroidery floss or craft thread, 2 feet

Directions

1. Pleat each piece of origami paper from corner to corner. The pleats should be narrow (about ½ inch).

2. Place the pleated papers together and wrap colored tape around the middle. The tape forms the butterfly's body.

3. Open the pleats on each side of the tape to form fans.

4. Use Glue Dots or a glue stick to glue the fans together at the sides to form wings.

5. Tie embroidery floss or craft thread to the top of the butterfly so that it can be hung as a decoration.

Julie Concentration

Play with a friend or challenge yourself to a game of Concentration. Punch out the cards and turn them all upside down. Flip over two at a time. If they match, you keep the cards. If you're playing with a friend, take turns trying to match cards. If you find a match, take another turn.

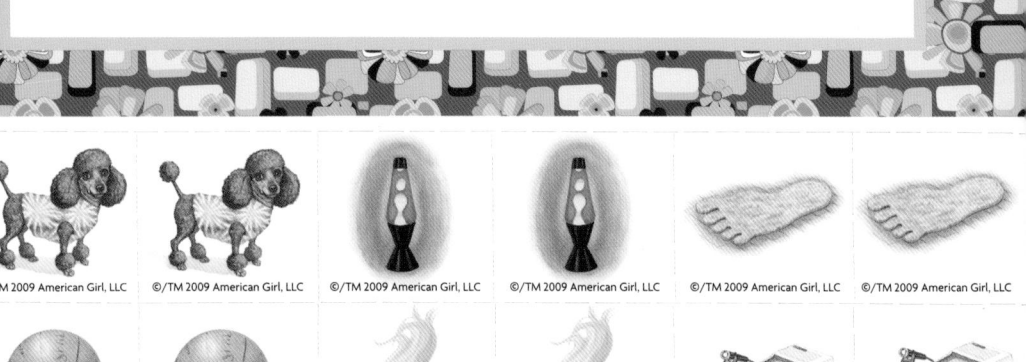

Make a Storage Box

Keep your Concentration cards in this cute storage box.
1. Punch out the box and make a crease along each dotted line.
2. Apply tape or glue to the marked area, and then fold the box.
   If you use glue, let the box dry before you put anything in it.

©/TM 2009 American Girl, LLC

Glue or tape
here.

Glue or tape
here.

Campaign Promise

Julie ran for student body president against Mark Salisbury, one of the most popular boys in school. If elected president, Mark promised everyone would get pizza for hot lunch in the cafeteria every Friday. What was Julie's campaign promise?

To solve the puzzle, place the letters above the purple line in the boxes below the purple line to form words. The letters in each column can be used only in that column. An orange square indicates the end of a word.

S	O	H	R	D	E	I	S	Y	T	I	O	N
F	C	A	O	O	E	T	S	E	S	T	O	M
I	H	R	N	G	L		E	H	E		E	
		P					T					

				M								
C												
			O							T		
							N					

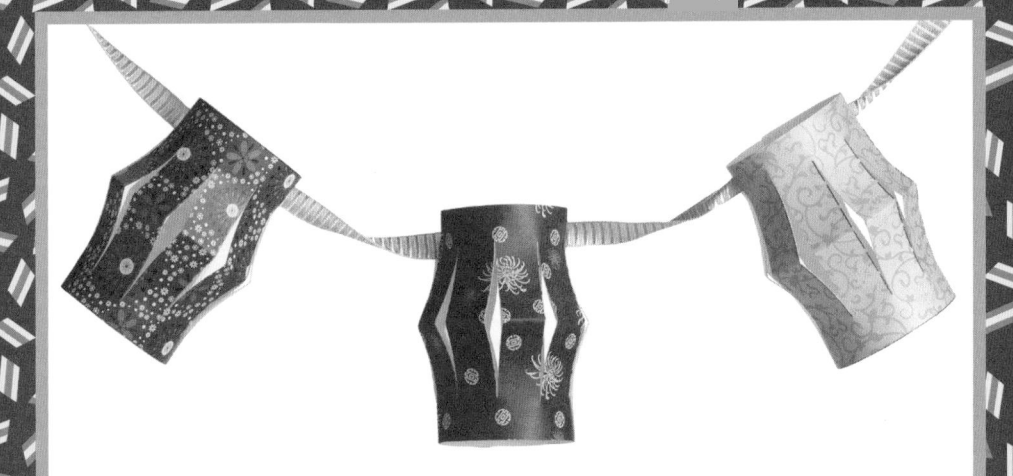

Make Mini Chinese Lanterns

Celebrate Chinese New Year—or any special day—
with pretty paper lanterns.

You will need:

- Tape
- String or ribbon
- Hole punch
- Scissors

1. Punch out the paper strips on the facing page.

2. Fold each strip in half the long way and make a crease.
   Cut slits along the dotted lines.

3. Unfold each strip. Roll the paper into a cylinder and tape ends together.

4. Use a hole punch to make a hole at the top of the lantern on each side.

5. Cut a 20-inch piece of string. Thread each lantern onto the string.

Stand Up, Charlotte!

Julie's older sister, Tracy, had to take care of Charlotte the spider plant for a class project. When Julie babysat for Charlotte one afternoon, she accidentally knocked the plant out the window! Julie quickly replanted Charlotte in a new pot and hoped Tracy wouldn't notice. Can you find two spider plants that are exactly alike?

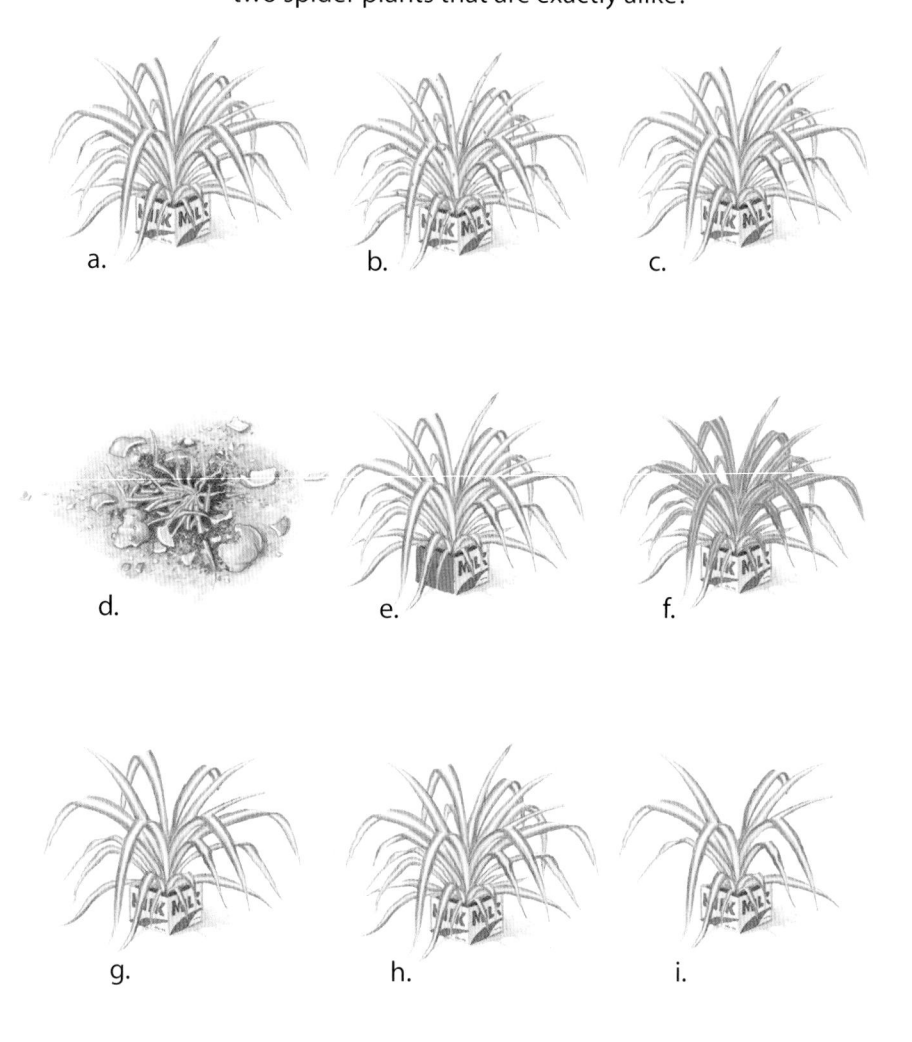

a.

b.

c.

d.

e.

f.

g.

h.

i.

Sticker Sudoku

Solve the Sudoku puzzle by using the picture stickers of Julie's feathered friends, a pair of bald eagles named Shasta and Sierra and their chick, Freckles. Fill in the boxes so that every row, every column, and every 2-by-3 rectangle has one of each of the six pictures.

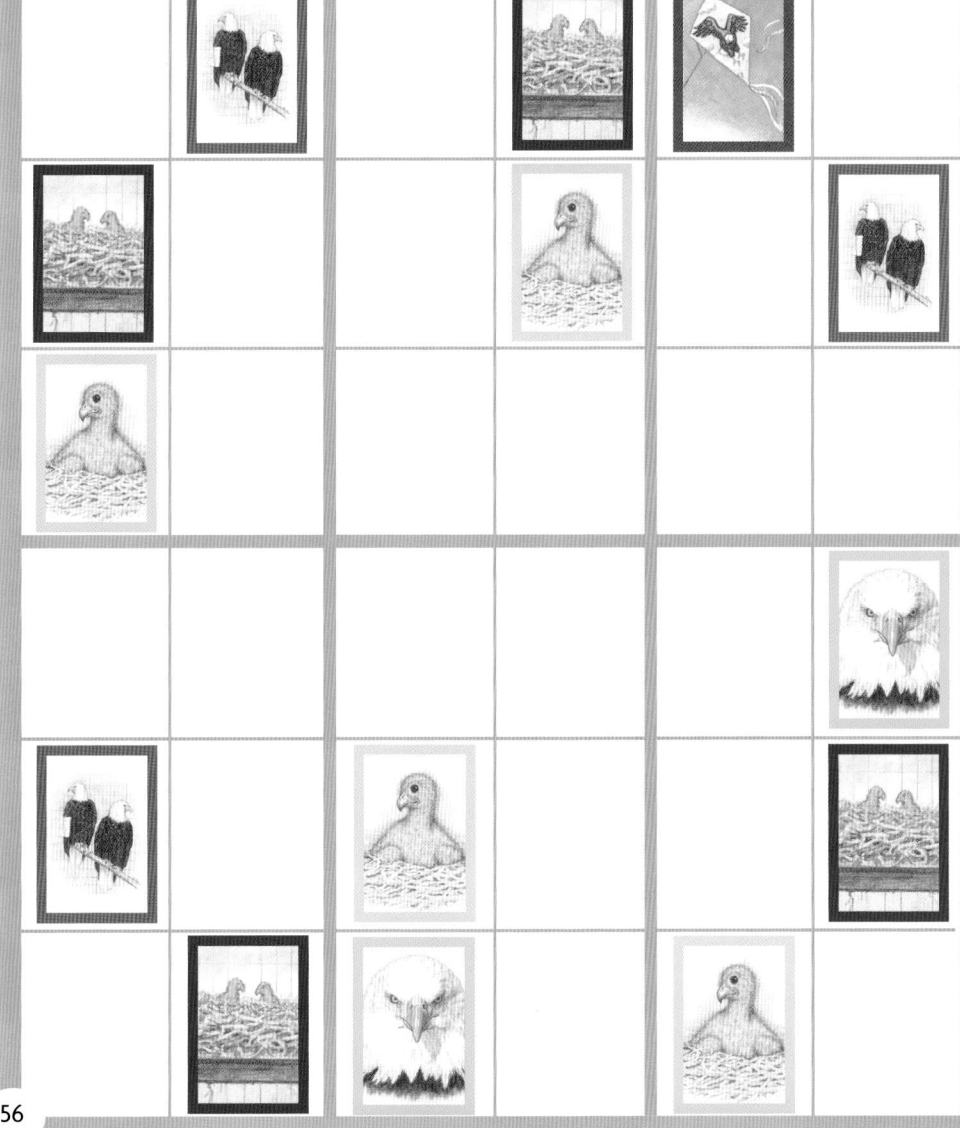

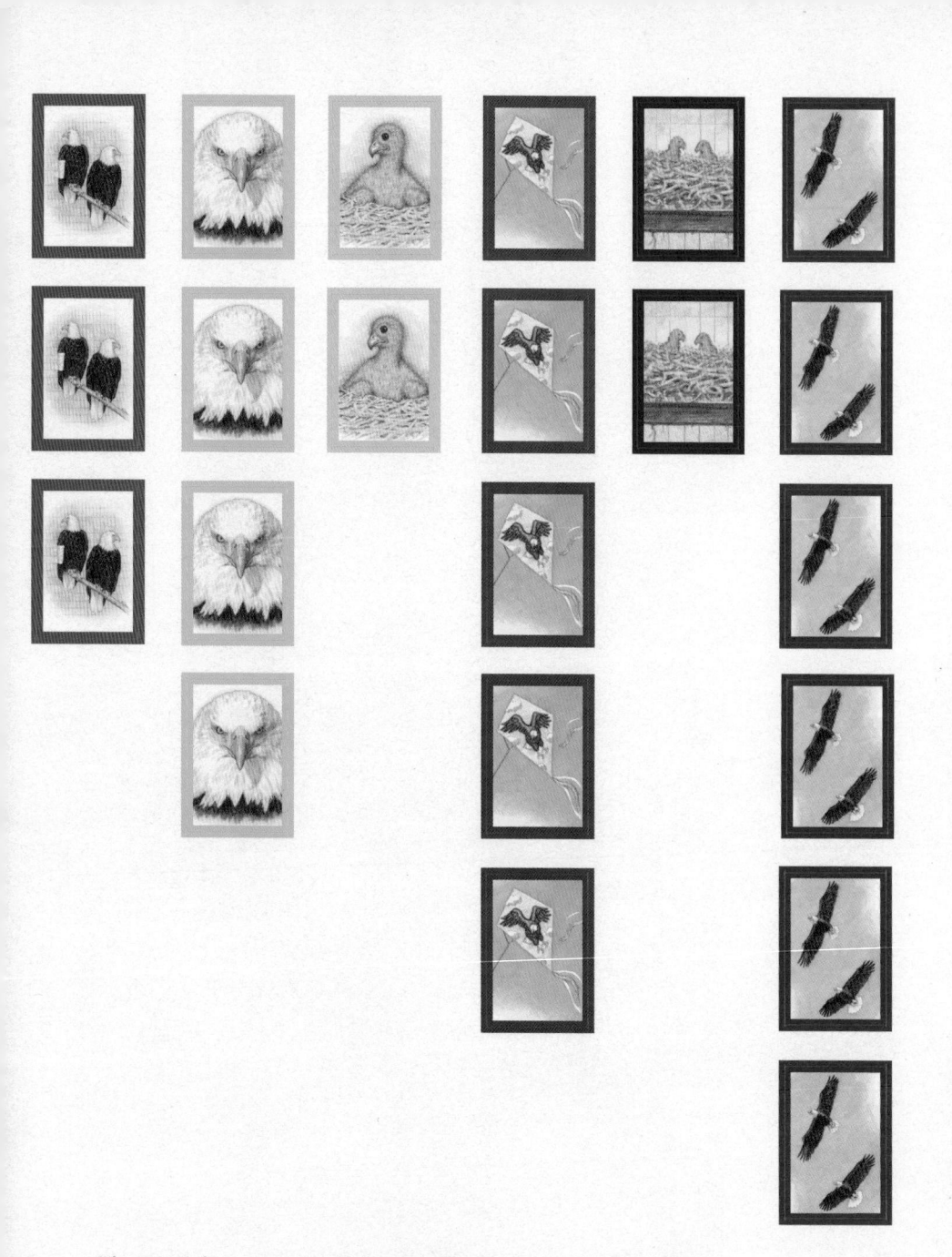

These stickers are reusable, so you can move them around
as you work the puzzle. When you've solved the Sudoku,
remove the stickers and pass on the puzzle to a friend.

Secret Signals

Julie's dad's house was right across the street from Julie's friend Ivy's house. Each night, the girls signaled good night to each other by blinking their bedroom lights ten times. It was their secret code for "Good night, sleep tight, don't let the bedbugs bite!"

You can use Morse code to send messages using light flashes or written-down dots and dashes. The dots are short flashes and the dashes are longer ones. Here's the code:

A	· —	N	— ·
B	— · · ·	O	— — —
C	— · — ·	P	· — — ·
D	— · ·	Q	— — · —
E	·	R	· — ·
F	· · — ·	S	· · ·
G	— — ·	T	—
H	· · · ·	U	· · —
I	· ·	V	· · · —
J	· — — —	W	· — —
K	— · —	X	— · · —
L	· — · ·	Y	— · — —
M	— —	Z	— — · ·

Wagons, Ho!

Julie celebrated America's Bicentennial by traveling across the country in an old-fashioned pioneer-style wagon train. Everything Julie and her family needed for the long journey had to fit inside their covered wagon. See if you can fit Julie's supplies into the cross grid.

Start by filling in the 9- and 11-letter words. There's only one place each of those words will fit. Then fill in the rest of the puzzle.

4 letters
FOOD
PANS
POTS
TENT

5 letters
BANJO
BOOKS
RADIO
TOOLS

6 letters
COOLER
FIDDLE
GUITAR
SADDLE

7 letters
BLANKET
HARNESS
JOURNAL

9 letters
MAGAZINES

10 letters
BOARD GAMES
FLASHLIGHT

11 letters
SLEEPING BAG

12 letters
HORSE BRUSHES
PIONEER DRESS

Basketball Word Search

Julie's going to play in a big tournament game against the Wildcats. Help her get ready by finding all the words in the list below.

```
O  G  D  V  Y  D  Z  E  V  F  F  T  H  B  E
H  M  H  E  K  F  C  C  L  O  O  D  N  A  H
H  V  H  F  F  I  R  B  C  R  U  F  M  F  B
H  C  P  A  T  E  O  P  B  W  L  R  I  K  W
I  A  A  C  Q  N  N  O  O  A  X  I  P  H  B
W  F  A  O  F  I  U  S  J  R  F  V  Y  M  C
P  R  T  U  C  N  G  B  E  D  K  D  N  H  M
P  A  S  B  C  T  E  K  S  A  B  R  I  M  I
L  X  S  E  Z  T  T  E  A  M  H  A  U  E  O
D  O  H  S  B  Z  C  W  K  O  G  U  F  J  L
D  R  I  B  B  L  E  N  O  N  O  G  A  S  G
C  Q  O  Z  C  D  U  P  Q  G  D  T  X  J  I
W  S  O  Z  K  D  A  L  K  E  R  O  Z  X  J
```

BASKET	DUNK	HOOP
BOUNCE	FORWARD	PASS
COACH	FOUL	PRACTICE
DEFENSE	GUARD	TEAM
DRIBBLE	HAND	

Flower Power

Make Gum-Chain Jewelry

At Gladrags, Julie's mom specialized in making decorative items from things other people might throw away. Try making a necklace or bracelet from ordinary gum wrappers.

1 Open wrapper.

2 Fold in half and open up again.

3 Fold bottom up to middle crease.

4 Fold top down to middle crease. Then fold in half.

5 Fold in half lengthwise. Fold ends in half toward the middle.

6 Make another link. Then slide the ends of one through the slots of the other. Add as many more links as you like.

For Two to Do

Julie and Ivy would have loved to play this game together.
You can play with a friend or family member. Discover how many details
you do—or don't—notice about each other.

Tear out the checklists on the next two pages. Keep one, and give the
other to your friend. Now sit with your backs to each other and answer the
questions. No peeking! When you've both answered all the questions,
turn around and check your answers.

What color are her eyes? _____

Is she wearing glasses? ☐ yes ☐ no

Is she wearing earrings? ☐ yes ☐ no

If yes, describe them. _____

What color is she wearing on top? _____

What color is she wearing on the bottom? _____

Are there buttons on her shirt? ☐ yes ☐ no

Do any of her clothes have pockets? ☐ yes ☐ no

If yes, how many? _____

Is she wearing something in her hair? ☐ yes ☐ no

Is she wearing a necklace? ☐ yes ☐ no

Is she wearing a watch? ☐ yes ☐ no

If yes, which wrist is it on? ☐ right ☐ left

Describe her shoes. _____

Is she wearing socks? ☐ yes ☐ no

If yes, what color are they? _____

Is she wearing fingernail polish? ☐ yes ☐ no

Are her toenails painted? ☐ yes ☐ no

If yes, what color? _____

What color are her eyes? _____

Is she wearing glasses? ☐ yes ☐ no

Is she wearing earrings? ☐ yes ☐ no

If yes, describe them. _____

What color is she wearing on top? _____

What color is she wearing on the bottom? _____

Are there buttons on her shirt? ☐ yes ☐ no

Do any of her clothes have pockets? ☐ yes ☐ no

If yes, how many? _____

Is she wearing something in her hair? ☐ yes ☐ no

Is she wearing a necklace? ☐ yes ☐ no

Is she wearing a watch? ☐ yes ☐ no

If yes, which wrist is it on? ☐ right ☐ left

Describe her shoes. _____

Is she wearing socks? ☐ yes ☐ no

If yes, what color are they? _____

Is she wearing fingernail polish? ☐ yes ☐ no

Are her toenails painted? ☐ yes ☐ no

If yes, what color? _____

Folding Puzzle

1. Tear the puzzle from the book.

2. Lift the top flap. Gently separate the four strips of paper.

3. Lift the second flap and separate those four strips of paper.

4. Discover the picture puzzle by weaving the paper strips in the correct order. After you solve one puzzle, undo the strips and solve the second one.

5. Turn over the card to solve two more puzzles.

Throw this section away.

☆ American Girl®

Julie

Buddy Bracelets

Julie and Ivy want to wear matching friendship bracelets.
Which two would they choose?

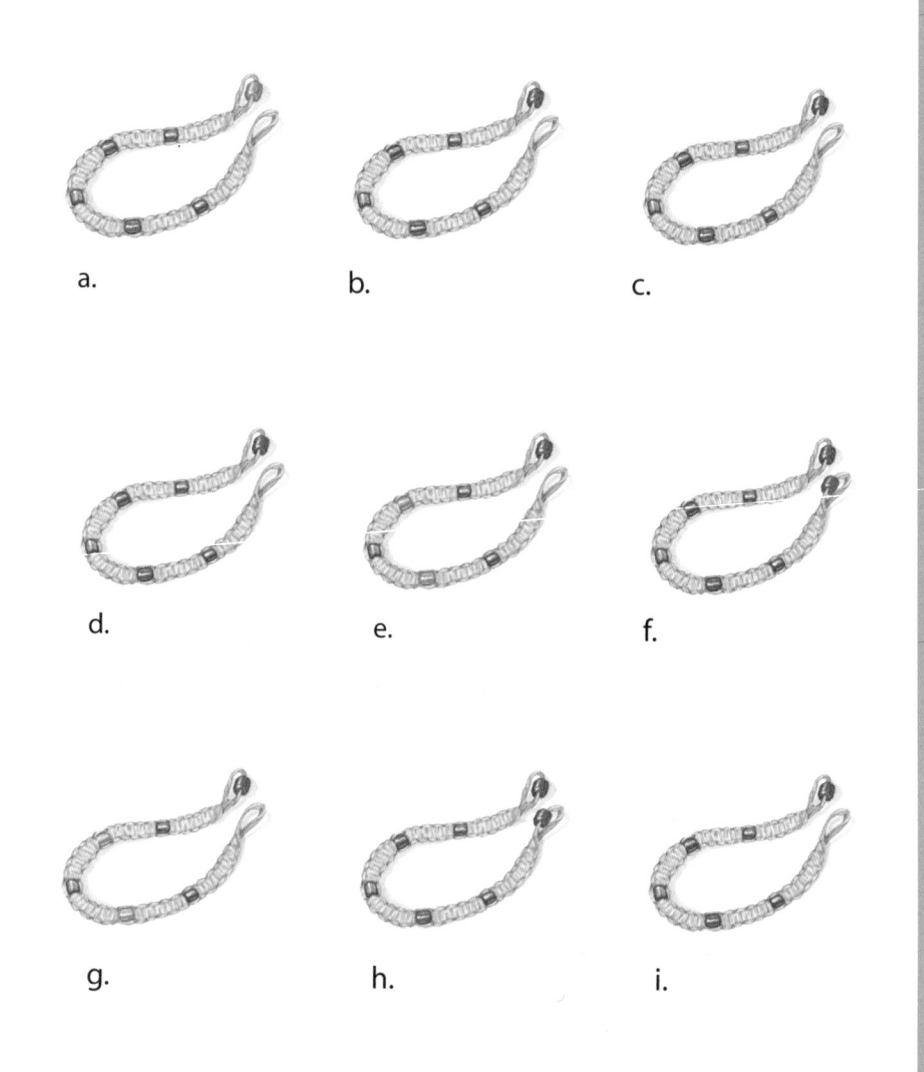

a.

b.

c.

d.

e.

f.

g.

h.

i.

Answers

PAGE 4

PAGE 7

acorn	corn	inns	scans
afar	crass	iron	scar
air	cross	is	scars
airs	fair	no	scarf
an	fairs	nor	scorn
arc	far	oaf	sins
arcs	fin	oar	sir
arson	fins	oars	sirs
as	fir	oasis	so
asia	for	of	soar
can	icon	on	soars
cans	icons	or	sofa
car	if	rain	sofas
cars	in	rains	son
coin	Inca	ran	sons
coins	Incas	sari	sonic
con	inn	scan	

PAGES 8–9

PAGE 21

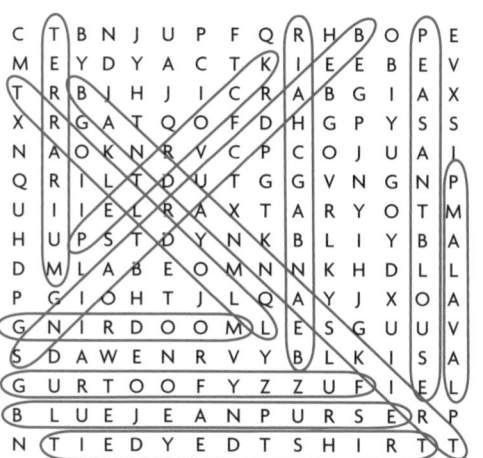

PAGE 22

C	T	H	L	D	E	S	O	I	H	E	L	R
M	O	U	E	Y	T	T	A	D	S	S	E	P
C	L	H	E	S		O	O	L	T	H	E	
	O	A	E			A			E	H		
	S	H	E			T	O	L	D		H	E	R
C	L	A	S	S			S	O		T	H	E	Y
C	O	U	L	D		R	A	I	S	E		
M	O	N	E	Y		T	O		H	E	L	P
T	H	E			E	A	G	L	E	S		

PAGE 23

75

Answers

SPLIT JUMP P

PAGE 27

UNEVEN BARS

BEAM

TUCK JUMP

DISMOUNT

PLIE

CARTWHEEL

MAT

ROUND OFF

STRETCHES

PAGES 28–29

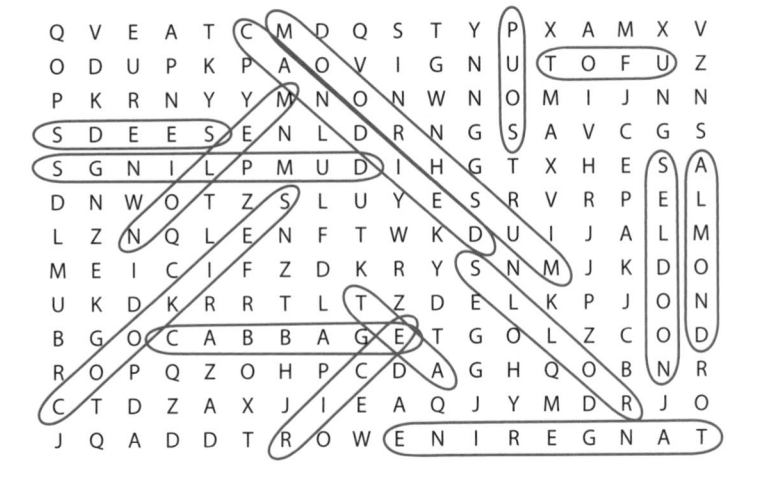

PAGE 39

abet	be	can	lain	net
able	bean	cane	lane	nice
ace	beat	cat	late	nine
acne	bee	cent	lean	tab
act	been	clan	lent	tail
ail	beet	eat	let	tale
an	belt	eel	lice	tan
ant	bent	ice	lie	tea
at	bet	in	line	teen
ate	bile	Inca	lint	ten
bait	bin	inn	lit	tile
bale	bit	it	nab	tin
ban	bite	lab	nail	
bat	cab	lace	neat	

PAGE 41

Start

Finish

PAGE 51

S	O	H	R	D	E	I	S	Y	T	I	O	N
F	C	A	O	O	E	T	S	E	S	T	O	M
I	H	R	N	G	L		E	H	E		E	
		P					T					

I		P	R	O	M	I	S	E		T	O	
C	H	A	N	G	E		T	H	E			
S	C	H	O	O	L		S	Y	S	T	E	M
F	O	R		D	E	T	E	N	T	I	O	N

Answers

PAGE 55

a.

b.

c.

d.

e.

f.

g.

h.

i.

PAGE 56

PAGE 61

PAGE 62

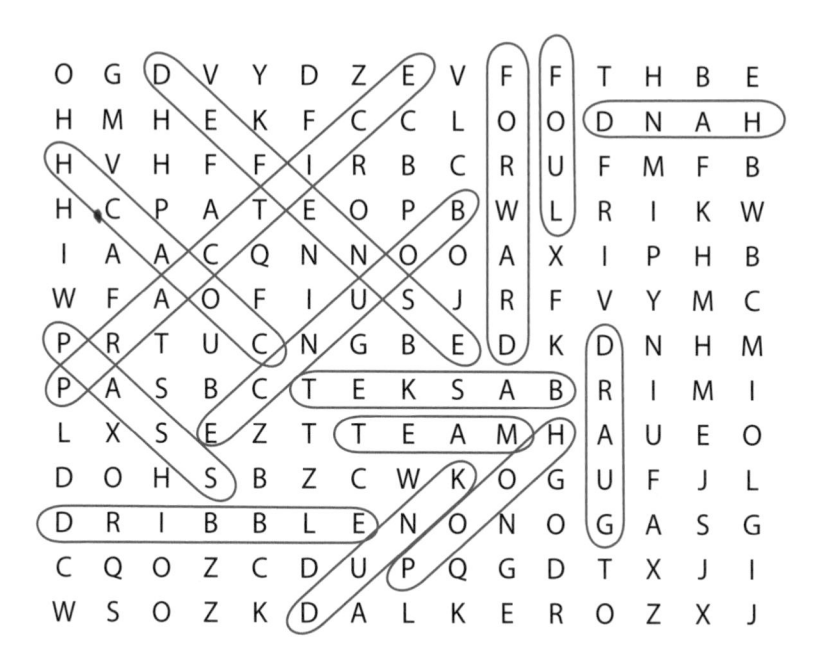

PAGE 73

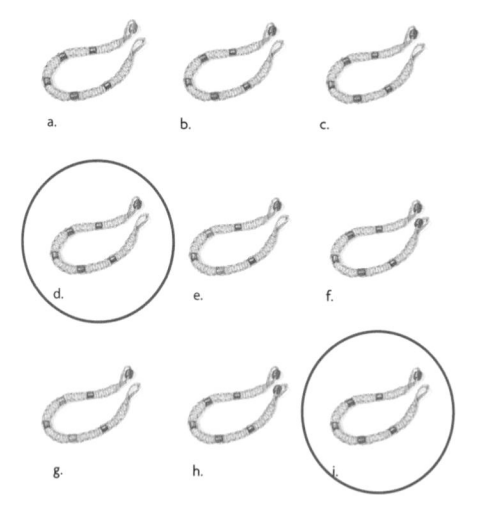

a.   b.   c.

d.   e.   f.

g.   h.   i.